Preface

This book started out as an email to my family after revisiting The Falkland Islands 31 years after the war in 1982 in which I was a part of. I have decided that the beginning of the book should be the original email because of the authentic nature in which it was started.

The people of the Falkland Islands have always considered themselves British Citizens and fly the British flag with pride. Their language and culture is British in every way.

1982 saw a lot of unrest in Argentina, inflation was at something like 1000% and the then leader of their "Junta", General Leopoldo Galtieri, needed something to unite the people and get them back behind him. For many years the Falkland Islands, known to the Argentinians as The Malvinas has been a topic of hot debate. They are situated about 310 miles off the Patagonian coast in the South Atlantic Ocean, about 8,000 miles from mainland UK. Argentinian claim over the islands has been of great importance to them. General Galtieri thought this would be a great opportunity to lay its claim on the Islands and sent an invasion force to the Islands on April 2, 1982. The plan worked at first, the anti-Junta demonstrations quickly turned to patriotic demonstrations.

The Prime Minister of the United Kingdom sent a task force south to return the Falkland Islands back to British rule.

Our Battalion, 1st Battalion Welsh Guards were selected to go as part of the second wave of troops, 5 Infantry Brigade. 3 Infantry Brigade had already been dispatched. It was kept secret until shortly before 12 May, 1982 when we boarded the cruise ship the QE2. We sailed south for several weeks and landed in San Carlos on June 2, 1982.

Included in my explanations of my revisit to the islands and the battle field tours, you will read true life accounts of some of the men who fought there. I try to give the feeling as much as possible of being in amongst the horrors of war, as it happened, and to the best of my research, in chronological order. Some facts may be slightly inaccurate but at no time have I embellished them with my own versions.

30 YEARS OF BATTLE

30 YEARS OF BATTLE

Copyright 2013

Andy Brinkworth

Dedicated to my old friend Bowser,

my fantastic wife Jennifer who I wake many nights with my crying out in my sleep,

all the brave men and women who fought and fight for our safety and freedom.

Hi everyone, I'm back and settled into Indy life (now living in Indiana, USA). I had a great trip, well worth the long journey, a lot of emotions, good and sad. I learned a lot of things I did not know about, as I have said before, when we (Falklands Veterans) get together we just have beer and fun, never talked about it. In amongst the ground, memorials and crosses are a different atmosphere and openness.

I would like to first remember those that made the journey south in 1982 for a very good cause, some never to return.

They called it a conflict, my interpretation of a conflict is a spat, a row, a disagreement......I could go on. For those that were there, there's no doubt, we were at WAR with Argentina. Calling it a conflict was a way of not being in a position of consequence.

Casualties and losses during this war

Argentina	UK
649 killed	258 killed
1,657 wounded	775 wounded
11,313 taken prisoner	115 taken prisoner

"THEY (The Falkland Islanders) **ARE FEW IN NUMBER, BUT THEY HAVE THE RIGHT TO LIVE IN PEACE, TO CHOOSE THEIR OWN WAY OF LIFE AND TO DETERMINE THEIR OWN ALLEGIANCE."** Rt. Hon. Margaret Thatcher, April 3, 1982

"THEY FLY THE BRITISH FLAG AND THEY DRINK BRITISH BEER."
Probably every British soldier that made the long journey south. 1982

Wed 30th Jan, 2013

We met up 30 years after the war at RAF Brize Norton, England, a group of Falklands Veterans about to embark on a pilgrimage 8000 miles south.

A long and tiring flight south with a 2 hour layover in Ascension Islands, in a DRY old airbus 330 run by a Portuguese airline. Couldn't even drink ourselves to sleep, they cut us off after two pints in Brize, they realized we were just meeting up after many years and they thought it could have got ugly!!!!!!! Whaaaaaat? Not us!!

<u>Thurs 31st Jan, 2013</u>

We arrived in Stanley and got ourselves situated in Liberty Lodge, fully built and now funded for veterans through charitable donations; it's a beautiful place overlooking Stanley harbour. Since it was built in 2006 not one veteran or family member has paid a penny for their stay.

Liberty Lodge, Port Stanley, Falkland Islands.

View of Stanley Harbour from the Lodge

I roomed with Billy Mott and his brother Nicky. The returning group of veterans numbered 10 guys, 8 Welsh Guards, 1 Scots Guard and 1 from The Royal Navy. After unpacking we all went into Stanley for a few beverages, visited a few pubs, not unlike the pubs of old that used to adorn every street in the docks of every town in Britain years ago, very quaint with wonderful people. This place is locked in a time-warp. We then went back to the lodge for a few more and some very funny stories of old. Then bed.

Fri 1st Feb, 2013.

After breakfast we were picked up by Land Rovers from Liberty Lodge in Stanley and taken on some battle field tours, we first visited Bowsers cross, for those of you that don't know, Bowser (Christopher Charles Thomas, '03') was like a brother to me when I was in the Welsh Guards, we were rarely seen apart from each other, we used to ride our motor bikes all over, some places we shouldn't have! He was sadly killed during the war. Our group leader Lt Col Tony Davies, (he was our Regimental Sergeant Major during the war, like a father to us all as he still is, we were HIS boys) explained how Bowser died, he was acting under orders from Tony on his motor bike, moving supplies to and from 2 Company's position south of Mt Harriet and the Royal Marines, the Marines had not long taken Mount Harriett during the night, this was at the base of Mt Harriett that spanned out to the sea where all that was really left of the Welsh Guards, was 2 Company waiting to take Sapper Hill. One of our returning veterans in our group was Jimmy Everett, he was the Company Sergeant Major of 2 Company and saw the demise of Bowser.

It was on the last day of the war before the surrender, I will get to the beginning and come all the way back to this battle later, I am mentioning this because we wanted to visit Bowsers cross as it's close to Stanley. As Bowser was riding between one to the other a shell hit him, his riding partner Sgt Eric Padmore ran to the top of the hill for help, there he could see where Tony was, in the craziness, din of the battle and the wind, got his attention by firing his rifle in the air several times, Tony and others knew something bad had happened and ran to Eric's assistance, they saw that Bowser was laying in big trouble, his bike was smashed to bits, you only have to imagine how Bowser looked, they got a chopper to come in to get Bowser out, unfortunately it was too late for him. They wrapped him up and got him to Fitzroy. This is a different story then I was told in 1982, maybe they were trying to shield me from the truth?????? This was a very emotional visit. **RIP my old friend**.

I wanted to share with others visiting the Islands of our young life together, I made a transparent box with two motor bikes parked side by side, as we often left them, a welsh flag and a plaque, I fixed it in place next to his cross in the place where he was killed, the plaque reads:

"Bowser"

A quest for living life on the edge must include a willingness to die.

Rest in Peace Brother.

The medal nailed above the horizontal of the cross was a gift from my wife Jennifer, it's a Harley Davidson medal with BOWSER engraved inside the HD sign, she, wishing she had met my friend.

There were always differing opinions on what actually killed Bowser, some say he was hit by a shell. The following is an eye witness account from John "Brummie" Maher, an Engineer from 59 Commando, Royal Engineers, he was mine clearing at the time, he says the following.

We had taken Mt Harriet the night before with 42 Cdo RM and if you have ever read about the battle you will know that the recce work prior to the attack which I was involved with, had established heavy minefields to the Mountain's front. This led to the attack on the mountain from the rear. Many prisoners were taken the next morning and after we had daylight, we (2Tp, 59 Cdo RE) set about doing some clearance to the north of the road/track at the foot of Harriet. There was a large crater in the road/track and suspected but not confirmed at that time would be booby traps. As land forces were getting prepared for the next set of attacks, Bowser arrived along the track on his bike, arriving at the crater he decided to drive around it on the South side and hit an antitank mine. In the minefield on the other side of the track we dived for cover as we were showered by debris from the blast. As I fell to the ground I still to this day remember seeing Bowser in the air and coming down into the minefield. Myself and a colleague Roy Gillon breached our way to Bowser who was still alive, but badly injured, as we dragged him out he held my wrist so tight I had to prize his hand from myself. One foot, lower leg had gone and the other just about attached, he was bleeding badly from the abdominal area. We dragged him from the minefield onto the track and was helped by the rest of the guys. He was still with us as we got a helicopter onto the track to take him away as your RSM explained above. The news relayed back that he never made it. RIP Bowser, a brave man.

Me, Tony, Billy and Nicky Mott, with Bowsers memorial. Mt Harriet in the background.

Bowser's grave in Pirbright Military Cemetery Surrey, England.

The Peak of Mt. Harriet.

From Bowser's memorial we ascended Mt Harriet where we saw first hand how hard it must have been for any of these mountains to be taken, the Argies were heavily dug into granite rocks, the ground between the rocks was very boggy and undulating, I'm sure if you didn't succumb to bullets, flying shrapnel from the shelling by our Artillery and Navy and the flying pieces of granite you would break or twist ankles while trying to shoot the enemy, there was also a lot of hand to hand fighting with fixed bayonets, all this at night after clambering up very steep and treacherous terrain.

We then went on to Mt Tumbledown, this was taken by the Scots Guards immediately after the fall of Harriet, a very similar battle by extremely brave Scotsmen, I'm sure that if they had been wearing kilts and painted blue faces the Argies would have quit before they advanced. One of our returning group was Ronnie Mackenzie, he was the RSM of the Jocks at the time, he laid a wreath and said some words for his fallen comrades, another very emotional time for us all, and I cannot imagine what sort of emotions were going through the minds of these brave men.

The top of Mt Tumbledown with Stanley in the background. Our group
with the Scots Guards Memorial

We returned to the lodge and changed into shirt and tie to visit
the Governor at Governors House for tea and scones with jam and
cream, he was impressed by our attire, he probably doesn't have many
visits from the Household Division!! A very nice man, he told us the
current state of affairs regarding the Argie's claim to the islands, as a
matter of fact, there is NO eveidence anywhere that they have EVER
owned the islands!! They will not become Argentinian, there are more

British flags on the Falklands including off the roofs of cars than in a city hosting the American Superbowl flying their team's flag.

We later went to the Malvina Hotel (named after a daughter of an original owner from Scotland, not the name of the Malvinas) where we partook in liquid refreshments and song, only the first verses though, all other verses were lalalala, haha.

Back to the lodge, more liquid and laughter, bed.

Sat 2nd Feb, 2013.

We visited 'Memorial Wood 1982', this is in Stanley and is dedicated to every fallen soldier of the war, a tree has been planted for each one and has his name at the base. We laid crosses at one or two Welsh Guards each, I laid one for Bowser and one for Jim Carlyle, Jim died right next to me, as did my gunner, 32 Gdsm Edwards and another of our section, Gdsm Marks on the attack of RFA Sir Galahad.

Entrance to Memorial Wood

Bowser's Tree

Jim Carlyle's Tree

Tony and Ben Parry relaxing in Memorial Wood.

That afternoon we watched Wales win the second half against Ireland, we won't say anymore than that! The first half of that game was our only sour point of the Six Nations Championship, we went on to retain the title.

That evening we hosted guests for curry and drinks at the Lodge, many of these have been very generous for the upkeep of the Lodge, more singing of the first verse and lalala the rest, we Welsh love our singing don't we?

When our guests left we had more liquid, banter and jokes....then bed.

Sun 3rd Feb, 2013

Today we headed out to the main landing point of the war in 1982, San Carlos where we came ashore on June 2nd. Our guides intended taking us through as many of the battlefields as the day would allow.

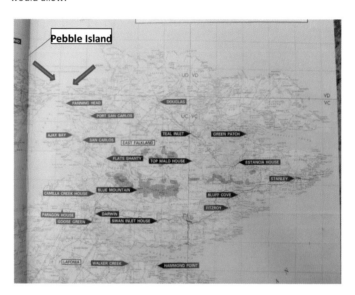

So back to 1982. In order for our Fleet to achieve safe passage into Falkland Sound and to the landing point in San Carlos, Falkland Sound is the body of water separating East and West Falkland, (marked between blue arrows) our Special Forces, the Special Air Service had to secure the area from any Argentine strongholds in the region. The following is the depiction of the Raid on Pebble Island on May 15th, 1982.

Pebble Island is a long and narrow shape Island that lies east to west across the western approaches to Falkland Sound. On 23 April, an Argentine aircraft landed on the airstrip there near the settlement which was home to the 25-strong farming community, supposedly to deliver the mail. One of the occupants of the aircraft surveyed the strip, walking some length along the main runway. A few hours later a UH-1 helicopter landed on the strip, depositing an Argentine Army patrol that then marched into the settlement and demanded that all radio transmitters of any kind be handed over. The leader of the soldiers stated that the occupying forces would send a patrol to Pebble Island from time to time, but otherwise they would be completely cut off from the outside world, a worrying prospect for the islanders as they would have no communications in case of emergency.

On the following day the initial statement regarding the future of Pebble Island was proved to be a lie. A Short Skyvan twin-engine transport aircraft of Prefectura Naval Argentina, the Argentine Coastguard, landed on the airstrip, and disgorged a large party of Argentine Air Force ground personnel. This was followed by a number of T-34C-1 Turbo Mentor training and light ground-attack aircraft from 4 Escuadrilla de Ataque, who began patrol and training flights almost immediately. Over the next week, stores and provisions were brought in, on 30 April the first Pucara twin-engine ground attack fighters from Grupo 3 de Ataque arrived on the strip. The airfield was now home to an estimated 150 Argentine personnel, and the local population was practically confined to their houses by these men, except for trips to gather food. The Argentine personnel were very nervous for three reasons, the strip and preparations were unfinished, the expected garrison of 400 troops was not in place, and they were expecting an attack by the British against what was now the only major Argentine position on West Falkland and its islands. They did not have long to wait.

On the night of 11/12 May an eight man patrol team from Boat Troop, D Squadron, 22 Regiment SAS were landed by Sea King on Keppel Island, south of the western end of Pebble. The helicopter landed between Mount Keppel and Cove Hill, screening the event from Argentinian forces on Pebble Island. The eight men were carrying canoes as well as their full equipment, and marched overland to a point near the abandoned airstrip on the eastern end of Keppel Island. Here an

Observation Point was set up to ascertain the movement of Argentine troops on Pebble, particularly in the area the SAS troopers intended to canoe across to. They remained here for twenty-four hours on watch, before continuing their journey by canoe on the evening of 13 May across the dangerous Keppel Sound. The current and tides in this stretch of water were extremely hazardous, but the team had been well briefed and avoided the worst of the difficulties. Immediately on landing on Pebble Island, a two-man team went forward almost half the length of the island to First Mount, which overlooked the airstrip and the settlement. An Observation Point was set up, and detailed surveillance began, locating the ammunition and fuel dumps, as well as the important radar equipment, which could detect any attempt at a concealed approach by the British Task Force. This indeed was the whole point of the attack, the radar and the Pucaras represented a serious threat, and had to be eliminated as the island laid close to the approach routes to the intended landing area.

The wind had risen during the day of the 14 May, and since it was intended that the main force to attack the airfield be landed by helicopter there was general concern about the ability of the Sea Kings to operate at long range. The task group of ships to support the attack was the aircraft carrier HMS Hermes, the destroyer HMS Glamorgan and the frigate HMS Broadsword. The three warships approached Pebble Island from the north as darkness fell on the night of 14 May, but HMS Broadsword's Sea Wolf system, the only long-range air defence for the group, became defective. HMS Broadsword fell further and further behind the line of advance in the terrible weather as her crew tried to fix the vital system. HMS Glamorgan slowly closed to within only seven miles of the coast of Pebble to provide naval gunfire support, and the incredibly valuable, and therefore vulnerable HMS Hermes closed to within forty miles of the coast, much closer than planned, to give the 846 Squadron Sea Kings a fighting chance in the high winds. Considering that Pebble Island was much closer to the Argentine mainland than any previous foray by the carriers, this was a calculated risk and a very brave maneuver. The party ashore radioed that all the targets had been identified with eleven aircraft on the airfield, and recommended that the raid take place that night. They marked out landing sites for the helicopters that would ferry the 48 troopers of D Squadron 22 Regiment SAS and one naval gunfire expert, and all was ready.

The Naval Gunfire Support Forward Observer (NGSFO) was none other than Captain Chris Brown RA from 148 Battery of 29 Commando Regiment Royal Artillery, the same officer who had performed no small wonders in the re-capture of South Georgia. He would be directing the 4.5 inch guns of HMS Glamorgan in direct support of the SAS raid. The Sea King HC4 pilots flew into the landing zone using passive night vision goggles and the SAS team split up into an assault group and support group to give covering fire. The landing had been delayed by the weather, and the troopers had a long march with their full equipment as well as the mortars and rounds for them. As a consequence the original plan to contact the settlers before the attack had to be abandoned as there was no time. The mortar base was set up, and the General Purpose Machine Guns (GPMGs) arranged to cover the approaches from the settlement and the settlement itself where it was known the bulk of the Argentine forces were taking shelter from the weather.

Early in the morning of the 15 May, HMS Glamorgan began delivering 4.5 inch shells at the rate of one a minute under the direction of Captain Brown. The GPMG teams opened fire and kept the Argentine troops pinned down in the settlement area, while their colleagues went to work on the airfield. Using plastic explosive with short fuses, the SAS teams led by Captain John Hamilton destroyed all eleven aircraft, six Pucaras, four Turbo Mentors and the Short Skyvan, as well as the radar installation, fuel and ammunition dumps. The aircraft were attacked with teams destroying the same area of each to prevent the Argentines from assembling flyable aircraft from canibalising the wrecks. With the resounding success of the raid, the teams began to withdraw at 7:45 in the morning. By this time, the Argentines had managed to organise a response, and a sharp firefight began. The officer rallying the Argentine troops was identified and promptly shot, and the counter- attack dwindled almost immediately. The withdrawal then continued almost unopposed, except for the detonation of a remotely controlled mine which was set off too late to have any real effect, but managed to slightly wound two of the SAS troopers. The entire force boarded their helicopters without loss, and returned to the Task Force, having crippled the base, and ended any threat it and its aircraft posed to the proposed landings.

This incredibly brave and calculated offensive gave a clear and safe passage for the Task Force to enter Falkland Sound on June 2, 1982.

Our present day route from the Lodge at Port Stanley (A) to get to San Carlos was along the northern part of the East Falkland Island, we drove from Stanley in the east along the red line towards Bluff Cove, half way between Stanley and Bluff Cove the road goes north (B) to the east of Mt Kent and Two Sisters towards Estancia House and Teal Inlet. The mountain range (the tan colouration on the island map) separates the island from north and south, we drove out along the northern route in the reverse of the Royal Marines and 3rd Battalion Parachute Regiment battle route, we later return on the mountain and southern route, this was the route I would have taken and in fact what was left of the Welsh Guards actually fought on this route.

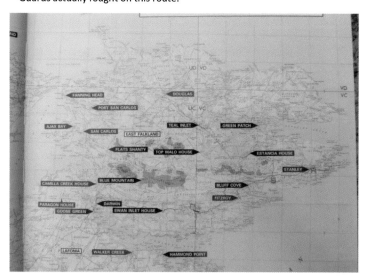

On the way out there we visited other battle sites, first of all was Mt Kent, this was one of the first mountain battles of the many before Stanley, it sits really at the beginning of the long mountain range leading up to Stanley. Mt Kent was actually occupied by Major Delves and about 30 men from the SAS, it was a major stronghold by the British with a good view in the distance of Stanley, they monitored troop movement by the Argies totaling around 7000 men. Several patrols were sent out to try to capture or kill the SAS without success, a full on assault by the Argies took place to try to capture the mountain at the end of May, this eventually resulted in the SAS surrounding the Argies to their demise, one of the enemy survivors were asked later why they didn't shoot back. He said "we would have if we could see anyone to shoot at!"

Present day Mt Kent is now an RAF listening post with radars and electronic equipment. On the slopes of Mt Kent are the wreckages of an Argie Chinook and Puma helicopter. On the 21st May 1982 two harriers were on patrol as dawn was breaking, they had no targets assigned but they knew about some aircraft on the slopes of Mt Kent, they flew over this patch of ground in very difficult light and had to make 3 passes, the first they were too low, the second they dropped their cluster bombs which missed, the third they had to use their guns which were successful, they took out the two and a third, a Huey flew off but crashed into the side of a mountain. This was the only Chinook the

Argies had left. When they got back to HMS Hermes one of the pilots, Squadron Leader Jerry Pook apologised to his wing man Flt Lt Mark Hare for making so many passes, Mark said, that's ok, didn't you see them shooting at us? Jerry said, what do you mean? Mark said, those troops by the Puma, they were shooting at us on every pass........in a classic RAF accent, Sqd Ldr Jerry Pook said, "Look old sport, do me a favour and tell me about that sort of thing next time will you?"

Wreckage of the Chinook. The rotor blade clearly states in spray paint
"MENDEZ - RTU".This would refer to the Argie Commander, General
Mendez, RTU means Return To Unit.

Wreckage of the Puma.

Along this route was Top Malo House and Estansia House, during the war we needed Estansia House in the north for an HQ base. Top Malo House was on the route and intelligence informed us that it was occupied by a platoon of Argies. 42 Commando The Royal Marines and 3 para moved along this route out of Port Stanley across very difficult terrain, the Marines sent in a patrol to take the house out, when they fired anti-tank weapons and grenade launchers into the house along with several rounds of ammunition, the Argies were jumping out of the windows, some were killed and the rest taken prisoner.

Next we came to Teal inlet, the Royal Marines and 3 Para pushed on through here to take the north route of the islands towards Stanley, their objective was to give support to the troops at Mt Kent.

Teal Inlet was used as a makeshift burial ground between 7th and 14th June 1982, twenty nine British soldiers were laid here from different parts of the war before later being moved to the cemetery in San Carlos and the UK.

The cross at Teale Inlet looking out to sea.

The cross at Teale Inlet showing the plaque with deceased names.

Our bus arrived at San Carlos, our destination this day from Stanley. This was our landing point from the ship SS Canberra and start point in 1982.

We were the second wave to land here as the Marines and Paras had done some weeks before, we landed at the jetty from our troop carrier, having disembarked from SS Canberra on 2 June 1982 and pressed on up the hill to dig in and await further orders. Our supply vessel Atlantic Conveyor had been attacked and sunk, that meant that our food, shelter and aircraft cover were lost, we had to beg borrow and steal but no one was willing to share, why would they, they needed it also.

Bowser, who sailed down on a cargo vessel before us, saw me come ashore, as I was walking up the hill, he ran up to me like a dog having been away from his master, he jumped on me, both of us falling to the ground and he stuffed a bottle of Bacardi into my jacket, Kean Rowlands, Al Bennett and I shared it that night, it was a great stress reliever to say the least.

We were dug in for a few days trying to stay dry and warm in the very wet and very cold South Atlantic wind and rain, San Carlos is known affectionately as "bomb alley", we often watched as Argie aircraft came in bombing our ships, it's amazing to see the power of a simple bomb that missed its target, shoot water into the air, way above what seemed to be the height of the mountains opposite.

San Carlos Bay, AKA Bomb Alley.

The landing jetty and the hills in the background where we dug in, also where Bowser gave me a gift!

Original photo of troops coming ashore on the jetty

Prior to us landing on the 2 June 1982, 2 Para (2nd Battalion Parachute Regiment) moved from here on 27/28 May to Darwin and Goose Green settlements. This battle will be explained as the battlefield tour reaches that point.

We the Welsh Guards were to walk to Goose Green on the night of the 5 June to help out 2 Para who had not long taken Goose Green and Darwin. It was about a 20 mile march, we were carrying about 120lbs of equipment apart from our ammunition and weapons, this was the case with all military personnel on the ground. Our heavy equipment such as mortars and anti-tank guns were being moved behind us with heavy vehicles. After walking about 10 miles our Commanding Officer, Lt Col Jonny Rickets found out that our heavy equipment was being bogged down with the weight in the peat bogs. We had the order that we were to turn around and go back, he was not prepared to go into a potential battle without this backup. So back we went

The next night we boarded HMS Fearless to sail around into Bluff Cove for the as mentioned support. Whilst on board I met up with Bowser again, this was the last time I would see him alive, we had some conversations, one of those was that he told me he didn't think he was going home, he wasn't scared of that fact, it was an acceptance to him and he was comfortable with that, I of course didn't take any notice of it...!!

We got into Bluff Cove in horrendous weather, the Scots Guards and our No2 Company got ashore after several hours of very rough seas in a landing craft, they were soaked through to the skin, it didn't help that they were also bombed from one of our ships, ouch, wrong coordinates, fortunately no one was hurt. We weren't able to get off and we returned to San Carlos. It was now the morning of the 7th June.

That night we had to board Sir Galahad, High Command decided they were losing too many Naval Vessels and couldn't afford to lose any more, even though HMS Fearless is designed for troop movement into battle zones, they decided to send us around on RFA Sir Galahad. When we got on board there was a huge hole right through the centre of the ship, she was hit by a shell earlier in the campaign but it didn't go off, the unexploded bomb was removed safely. What was funny when we boarded was that people were saying, 'well, lightening doesn't strike the same place twice'!!!!! Tell that to Lee Trevino (for you non golfers, he was a pro that has been struck by lightning on two separate occasions whilst playing golf).

This was the hole from where the bomb was removed.

We arrived at first light on the morning of 8th June 1982, it was a beautiful cloudless day, I was worried that we were going to be attacked if we did not get off, Kean Rowlands and I joked as the hours wore on that we watched an Exocet missile coming, we were in fact genuinely concerned but what do you say, "I'm outa here?" We were sat in Fitzroy Bay, not Bluff Cove where we should have been, (apparently another cock up on coordinates) Bluff Cove was the next inlet around the coast, it would have been a forty mile march from where we were if we got off the ship, (the bridge between Fitzroy and Bluff Cove had been blown by the Argies, it would only have been 10 miles across that, little did everyone know that the bridge had actually just been repaired by then) our Company Commanders, Major Guy Sayle and Major Charles Bremner wanted to be taken around to Bluff Cove on the ship and refused to get off. They had a heated argument with Major Ewen Southby-Tailyour of the Royal Marines, he was going mad because they wouldn't take his advice on how dangerous it was for us all to be on board this ship, they would not heed his warnings, and they would only take an order from someone higher than a Major!!!!!!

As morning broke, an Argie lookout on the peak of Mt Harriet could not believe his eyes when he saw Sir Galahad next to Sir Tristram, both at anchor unloading supplies, he got word to the mainland and an air strike was put into action, 5 planes were inbound to attack the two ships sitting quietly in Fitzroy Bay.

12 HOURS later as we were preparing to get off the ship (as it happens for the third or fourth time, I can't remember now, but each time being told to stand down), we were in the tank deck deep down inside the ship at the stern (back) when a very loud whoosh above us rocked the ship, Company Sergeant Major Williams 500 (since committed suicide, RIP 500) shouted "get down", he saved many lives that day. I flew down onto the deck as quickly as I could, as I did a huge blast of flame hit me in the face, I turned my head away from the blast but it was there too, I realised I was in a huge fireball and in big trouble, I stood up, it was quiet, very peaceful, (I assume because of the lack of oxygen inside fire, I remember the days of Physics class in school, sound cannot travel in a vacuum) I could see silent chaos all around me, people on fire, red, hot, silence, I wondered how long it would take for me to die as I knew I was going to, I thought of how sad my mother is going to be, I felt no pain at this point, I can only assume the human body relieves you of that when it gets to a certain level, then the fireball seemed to escape through the hatch in the roof of the tank deck, fortunately they had that open as they had been unloading supplies all day.

Shame it wasn't us that were being unloaded!!

I was now engulfed in thick black smoke and some parts of my combat jacket were on fire, I brushed my hand over them to put them out and the skin came away in strands, hanging from my hands and fingers like thin rags, now I could feel the pain, if you have ever burned yourself with a hot ember or catching your hand on the inside of an oven or the like, this seemed 1000 times worse. I remember there was a huge mountain of mortar rounds in boxes waiting to be pulled out, a bomb landed next to it but did not explode.........wow. Now it was all black, thick black smoke, acrid and hard to breath but I had no choice, I saw in the darkness lots of fires, I'm sure a lot of them were soldiers. I am alive, I know I have to get out, there are bullets cooking off now and ricocheting all over the place, for some reason I didn't want to get hit in the arse and I remember trying to pull my butt in to escape the bullets, the way out is through a small door on the side, there are now loads of guys trying to get through, I still had my webbing on (ammunition pouches etc), I managed to undo the belt with my now raw hands and discarded it so I wasn't taking up much room trying to get out, I eventually got into the stairwell, everyone was shouting "don't panic", this very much calmed the situation down and we moved through pretty quickly considering the situation, the stairwell was also full of think black acrid smoke. As I got to the top of the stairs and into the fresh air I realized what is meant by "sweet fresh air", I gasped in as much as I could, Kean called me from behind, he was about 3 guys back, at least he was alive, I was very grateful for that. I was told to go to the front of the ship and wait for a helicopter, the ship by now was exploding with very deep cruuummmps from below that felt like earthquakes, I didn't know how long this was going to last before the whole thing went up, now, I hate to say, it's every man for himself as I was in no way able to help anybody else, I wasn't going to hang around to be blown up again, I thought that I could get down the rigging into a lifeboat, let the helicopters take the ones that can't, besides, I don't how long I would have to wait and the longer I wait the more chance this baby is going to blow. A good friend and fellow Welsh Guardsman Dai Graham was carrying guys down the rigging on his back, then he would climb back up for another, he wanted to carry me, as strong as he is I didn't want to be swimming in the ice cold South Atlantic water, I took my chances and was able to put my arm through each hole so that my hands didn't have to grab the ropes, every now and again the rigging would bang against the side of the ship, man that was painful. I got into an orange inflatable life raft, I was treated by a medic that was on there, he put field dressings on my hands. It was so painful, blowing them seemed to ease the pain, there were other guys in the same situation so we were all just blowing each hand in turn, I almost fainted at one point through hyperventilation so I had to ease up a bit. The medic also gave me morphine. When morphine is administered in the field, the recipient has an 'M' drawn on the forehead, I could not have this done because the skin would have just come away, he wrote it on a tag and tied it to my jacket zipper. I could see the Galahad ablaze through the entrance to the lifeboat, I could not believe that I was on board that ship, there were huge explosions coming out of the hold, that's where I was. I hoped that we get as many off as we can, I feared for the rest of my fellow Welsh Guards and others who were on board.

RFA Sir Galahad in flames in the background

I was below deck under the hatch where these flames are coming from.

Inside the life raft is a cardboard tube with survival supplies, it should have had paddles but of course there were none, I don't know why as this is a sealed unit till its inflated, some guys that were not burned used the butt of their rifles to try to paddle to get us away from the ship and to shore, very slow going as the butt is only a couple of inches wide, they might as well have been using a dinner knife.

We did eventually make it to shore, when I got out I was greeted by a Para, one of many, he wanted to know if I had morphine, I had to explain that I had and didn't want any more, I showed him my tag. I was then escorted to a snow cat and got in the back, it took me to a medical station temporarily set up in a farming community before being put onto a helicopter and flown to HMS Intrepid, sister ship of HMS Fearless, I have no idea to this day where the ship was, probably back in Sweet home San Carlos.

Me just coming ashore explaining that I had been
given morphine already.

Both this photo and the one before were taken from video footage
from the BBC, hence the poor quality.

Two pics above are present day where we were taken before
being flown to HMS Intrepid

I was treated by one of the sailors from HMS Intrepid, all the Ships Company double up as medics for situations like this, we were in what seemed to be their canteen, it felt like there was a hundred of us at different tables being treated, I'm sure it wasn't that many. My clothes were cut off as I couldn't get my hands through the sleeves, my hands were cleaned and the dead burned skin cut away, flamazine cream was applied and then my hands put into plastic bags to keep the cream on and infection out. During this time we were taken to a waiting room where we were laid on camp beds and monitored, within minutes the ship's Captain announced that enemy aircraft were heading our way, we were all covered head to toe with a blanket.........not again, I can't go through another explosion. The Captain gave a running commentary, '80 miles out, 70 miles out, 60......' Then the ship shuddered as a sea dart missile was deployed, Captain tells us that the missile is on its way to greet them, 50 miles out, 40..... 'One of Dago airlines just disappeared off the radar screen, his buddy just said goodbye to his wingman and is now high tailing it back to Argentina.' All sent over the ships loud speaker for all to hear.

Later that day we were flown to the hospital Ship SS Uganda, 155 soldiers were taken on board injured that day, the nurses were overwhelmed with every kind of emotion there could possibly be, if you want to be a nurse this will be how you find out whether it's for you or not.

I was put in a bunk with my friend Paul Cunliffe who had the biggest bruise on his butt I have ever seen anywhere, an anti-tank gun must have been blown through the ship and hit him in the arse, his bruise was in the perfect shape of the back end of an 84mm Anti-Tank gun.

We joined two sailors from HMS Coventry, luckily for us they had been in the hospital before us, every evening in good old British Military tradition we were allowed one can of beer ration a night. One of these matelots (nickname for a sailor) told the nurse that was carrying a case of beers for distribution that a doctor wants her in the next ward, she huffed and asked him to watch the case of beer till she came back, she put it down on the floor and left, he smiled at us and slid it with his foot under his bed. When she came back she had another case as she had completely forgotten about the first one, that night was the first time the pain from the burns didn't hurt....cheers!!!!

During my time on SS Uganda, it may have been day 2 or three, I can't remember, I woke one morning and couldn't see, I was very scared but realized that my eyes were swollen shut, when I was eventually able to see through very narrow slits I realised that my face was as big as a football from the swelling. The swelling did eventually go down. Sleeping was difficult enough through the pain but when you lay on your pillow and can smell burned hair and flesh every night was awful.

I don't know how long we were on Uganda but we were eventually transferred to a survey ship, HMS Heckler, this vessel is apparently only supposed to sail about 4 miles offshore, we are in the middle of the South Atlantic Ocean with her. This took us on a very rough voyage for 4 days to Montevideo in Uruguay, the north side of River Plate, the south side of River Plate is Argentina! During my 4 day cruise we were often made to lay on our bunks because the weather was so bad, chairs that had come loose from their harnesses flew across the decks along with cups and jugs, nothing could be done till the weather calmed down, one time when I was laying on my bunk, the bed above mine which was hooked against the wall, came loose and crashed down onto its base, my hands were above my chest to keep them elevated so as not to throb so much, the bed crashed onto my hands......arggghhh.

When the weather did calm down we were able to walk around and see how our other colleagues were doing, you really find out who your real friends are when it's time to go to the toilet, hands that are wrapped in plastic bags is like not having any hands at all, they are really no use. I will leave the rest to your imagination, save to say, yes, No1 and No2 is impossible!

We eventually reached our destination where we were taken to the airport and got an RAF flight back to the UK. Our first hospital was RAF Wroughton in the West Country, my family came to visit me which was very emotional. I also later had a visit from Drum Major Carran, I saw him come into the ward and walked down the middle, I knew he was coming to me and I knew why, even before he got to my bed. He told me Bowser had been killed. I froze and didn't know what to do or say, of all the guys that had departed during this war, my best friend Bowser is gone. I will never see him again. I dreamed a lot about him for a long time after that, with great sadness waking and knowing it was just a dream.

We were then driven in an old Army bus for hours to the East side of London to Woolwich Military Hospital. The sun was shining brightly through the windows like a greenhouse, there was nowhere to put your hands away from the hot rays. We were at Woolwich hospital until we could make a fist with our healing hands. When I painfully managed it I was able to go home, my brother Dave and sister Kay came to collect me. We eventually arrived back home in South Wales to a homecoming party thrown by the village I grew up in.

Our house in Llandough, South Wales.

Dad's cousin Avril and her two kids Caroline and Robert. Avril has since passed away in a terrible car accident.

My first beer back home.

Mum, Dad, Dave, Kay and Dawn.

Back to 2013 and San Carlos. We visited our beach head and the jetty where we came ashore.

It wouldn't hold one person today, let alone an Army, we soaked up the memories. We also went to pay our respects at the cemetery, now a very poignant location housing several fallen heroes.

Derek 'Smokey' Cole, RN. Bill Mott, Welsh Guards.

Tony Davies, WG. Andy Brinkworth, WG.

Ron McKenzie, Scots Guards. Ben Parry, WG.

Chris Hopkins, WG. Nicky Mott, WG. Jimmy Everett, WG. Charlie

Carty, WG.

We drove from here to Darwin and Goose Green. We saw the Community Centre where 120 Falkland islanders were held, with only one toilet between them for two weeks.

Going back to 1982, 2 Para left San Carlos to take Darwin and Goose Green late in May, walking along that terrain is difficult enough as its boggy, undulating and large grass tufts are perfect for twisted ankles. Add in that it's cold, rain and strong winds, it's cold enough to snow but it's freezing rain instead. Now when you walk in single file as a Battalion, it's really difficult to get the speed consistent throughout from the man at the front to the man at the back, you walk fast at one point finding it hard to keep up and stopped at other points and your sweat starts to freeze. On the way to Darwin and Goose Green they encountered a land rover coming along the track in front of them, it was about 150 metres away, they thought it might be a local but weren't sure, they got in to the side of the track and got down, the sun was shining on the windshield so they couldn't see inside, then it stopped and the driver got out, as he was doing so they saw that he was wearing a military helmet, they opened fire. They killed two of the Argies form this land rover and injured two, these had to be treated for wounds whilst they were taken prisoner. This land rover incident is significant as you will see further on.

The Commanding Officer Lt Col H. Jones had given his orders that Darwin and Goose Green would be taken and re-organising on the other side in 6 hours. Prior to getting to the start line before the attack, Colonel H had heard that the BBC World Service had announced to the world that John Knott, MP had told Parliament that day that 2 Para were about to attack Goose Green, Colonel H went nuts.

The commanding Officer of the Argentinian 12 Infantry Regiment holding Goose Green, stated some time later that he had heard that news item on the World Service but thought they were playing a psychological battle, who would tell of an impending attack! It made no difference, he had read many books about the British Army including many about tactics now and during the Second World War. He said 'I knew an attack was imminent, particularly as I knew our patrol with the land rover wasn't coming back, I knew through these historical books that the British would attack with skill and at least the necessary strength and probably more, I did not think we could hold out for long.

The Argies we're dug in in several different locations, each location was a very hard fight, several different battles, some at the same time. All this time Colonel H was getting frustrated that his 6 hr time period was taking too long, lives were being lost, several injuries, organization was going out of the window, chaos started to ensue, H was getting angry! H joined one of the attacks to find out what was taking so long, why weren't they pushing on? They couldn't, they were pinned down by trenches with thousands of rounds of ammunition, they were in a gulley with enemy above them, they had to keep their heads down or risk it being shot off. H decided they couldn't stay there, they needed to move and he shouted "come on, let's go" H got up and charged the trenches, unfortunately there were more trenches than they knew about, they took out some and there was one that was strong, hard to take out, he headed a charge on that trench with others firing and attacking it, unfortunately a trench to the left was not seen and H was hit in the back, he fell at the trench he was attacking, the occupants were killed and H was laying on top dying.

Reinforcements arrived and the situation was controlled but too late for 2 Para Commanding Officer, attempts were made to patch him up but sadly Lt Colonel H Jones died. Commanding Officers are not supposed to lead a charge......unless you are H Jones and they are not supposed to get killed. He was later posthumously awarded the Victoria Cross, the highest award for valour, his wife Sara has it loaned to the National Army Museum in London.

Colonel H is buried with two of his men in San Carlos Cemetery. This obelisk has been built on the site that he fell.

The site where Col H was killed, the arrow is the obelisk, the photo is taken from where the trench was situated that was believed to have killed him.

There were several different battles going on all over Goose Green, some Argies would surrender and were taken back to Battalion HQ where they were dealt with as Prisoners of War.

An act of surrender by waving a white flag is in the rules of the Geneva Convention, the soldier surrendering is to be given safe harbour, and the soldier accepting the surrender is to be treated as friendly. One particular incident involved number 12 platoon with their Platoon Commander Lieutenant Jim Barry, some of 12 platoon saw some white flags being raised by the Argies, Lt Barry went forward with Lance Corporal Nigel Smith and Corporal Paul Sullivan to accept the surrender, he was seen remonstrating with them to put down their weapons, he put his against the fence and the Argies who were in trenches behind opened fire killing the three men. The rest of C Company opened fire on these Argies killing almost all.

In the words of a great man, Surgeon Commander Rick Jolly, OBE, (Senior Medical Officer, head surgeon at Ajax Bay, our version of M.A.S.H.) "This is the paradox of war. We can admire our enemies; we can even respect their courage and skill, but also cheer when they are removed violently from the Battlefield.

There is in fact another version to this story, told by both sides, there seems to be some discord as to whether white flags were waved or was it some net curtains seen waving in the window of the house behind. Nevertheless, two Argies walked forward with their hands in the air, some others were sat on the ground behind, also with their hands in the air, and one would think this is giving up. The commander of this group of Argies was Gomez Centurion, he was reputed to be a real hard arse, this version puts him as one of the negotiators, it appears he was thinking the Paras were giving up, when he realised they were wanting him to give up, he was heard to shout (he spoke good English, his father was military attaché in Washington DC) "son of a bitch (apparently, his favorite line)! You have got two minutes to return to your lines before I open fire. Get out!" Machine gun fire came overhead and all hell broke loose, Lt Barry was hit at point blank range and died instantly.

As a result of the loss of Col H, Major Chris Keeble assumed command of 2 Para, the remainder of the Battalion had to reorganise, they decided to 'stop fighting for the day' and had to regroup in the dark. They continued fighting after the re-org and fought through, way longer than Col H's very optimistic and detrimental 6hrs, it lasted for more than 24hrs.

This first battle on the ground to regain the Falkland Islands was a significant breakthrough, not only for morale but for British strategic positioning. Darwin and Goose Green were seen to be a poorly defended and weak opposition, this was so far from the truth. At the end of the battle some 1,200 Argies surrendered. 120 interned Falkland Islanders were released.

Unlike the movies where a battle is fought and won, soldiers move onto the next one.....here, the fallen have to be taken care of, there is no rear guard that follows to clean up, we have that job to do. There is no time to rest for these guys, a large mass grave was dug by the Falkland Islanders using tractors, the dead were identified and a battle death certificate issued for each of the fallen, they are then prepared for burial and a funeral service is conducted by friends who were fighting alongside these men only 24hrs earlier. No one could imagine the feeling, only those that were there will know.

We ended our visit to Darwin and Goose Green with a visit to the Argentinian Cemetery. A sad place in a different way, most of the graves here are of fallen that were 'not welcome back' in Argentina.

2 Para were later tasked with the job of heading out to Fitzroy, a mere 40 miles walk, "are you fucking pissed?" was one of the responses when they were told. Using the one Chinook they had left was a good alternative to ferry as many troops as possible, the problem obviously is as big as these aircraft are, they couldn't move the whole Battalion. They had to figure out if they were going to receive an Argie reception party in Fitzroy. They tried calling ahead to Fitzroy or Bluff Cove, there is a connecting bridge between both, if the Argies haven't blown it, it would save a 40 mile walk between the two. The phone line between Burntside House and Darwin was not working so Major John Crossland and Colour Sergeant Alan Morris got a helicopter ride to Swan Inlet House, the next farm away. No one was at the house so they had to break in, the phone system is a simple handle crank phone, they cranked the handle and a 13 yr old girl answered, Michelle Binnie, she didn't recognise the English accent on the other end and handed it to her father, Mr Binnie heard the voices on the other end announce,

'This is the British Army, can you talk freely?'
'Yes!' replied Ron.
'Are there any Argentinians near you?'
'No, they blew up Fitzroy Bridge and left'
'Fine, we will be with you shortly'.

After the call had been made it was decided to airlift 2 Para to Fitzroy and Bluff Cove. The load master on the Chinook said that in peace time only 40 men were allowed on the aircraft, the Company Sergeant Major yanked him out and said, well that's one less then. 80 men were loaded in a standing room only situation aboard the Chinook and a frantic dusk airlift took place, thus the first of the southerly advances by the British began. They occupied Fitzroy and Bluff Cove. This was June 2, 1982, the same day as we came ashore at San Carlos.

This was all in the south of the island, movements of troops to this region was outlined earlier with the walk of the Welsh Guards, then the subsequent ship journeys by the Scots Guards and Welsh Guards culminating in the disastrous outcome of the Sir Galahad and Sir Tristram on the 8th June.

June 3rd, Mt Wall, which was very close to the front line of the Argie defensive positions, British troops held this mountaintop and were using it as a rebroadcast station, (rebroadcast stations are used when working in mountainous terrain, radio signals struggle in this type of field so a rebro stn is set up to help the signal from point A to point C, the rebro stn being point B in between usually on high ground). Very high tech and expensive equipment was being used, it was also a great vantage point for observations of troop movements and fire control from our artillery.

A British patrol was in front of the rebro stn, which is a normal form of protection, when they heard an Argie patrol approaching, there was no alternative but to engage them at once so as not to involve the observers in the rebro stn. Four of the enemy were killed instantly by a withering burst of machine gun fire, a fifth was taken out by a sniper as he tried to scuttle vainly amongst the rocks, two or three others ran off down the mountain back towards the road.

Argie artillery fire now rained down on this mountain, the rebro team had to bug out fast and in doing so they had to leave their equipment and expensive laser target marking kit, before doing so they had to destroy it. The Argies got to the position and found the equipment left behind but surprisingly they did not use many men to take the mountain thus the British managed to take it back with ease shortly afterwards.

On the same day, to the north of the island, 45 Commando Royal Marines were setting off from Teal Inlet on their epic journey to Bluff Cove Peak, they covered it in a day. The British are moving up!

On the night of the 5th June a rebro station, which was set up on Pleasant Peak at Wickham Heights midway between Goose Green and Bluff Cove, was having some technical difficulties. In the early hours of the morning of the 6th June a gazelle helicopter piloted by Staff Sgt Chris Griffin and co-piloted by L/Cpl Simon Cockton, both of Army Air Corp, left with Major Mike Forge and Staff Sgt John Baker of the Royal Signals to rectify the situation. Meanwhile out at sea HMS Cardiff was monitoring air movement from the Argies with orders to disrupt their supply route into Stanley, the radar operator saw something moving in the air and didn't recognise it, he immediately thought, not knowing there were any friendly aircraft in the area, reported it and 2 Sea Dart missiles were dispatched. It was thought that an Argie Hercules was coming into Stanley or even a Hercules transporting Special Forces, nonetheless it was a Blue on Blue! (Blue on Blue is friendly fire killing your own) All four crew member were killed instantly. Enemy surface to air missiles were blamed. An inquiry revealed 4 years later that it was actually HMS Cardiff that struck the fateful blow. I think the crew knew deep down it was them, they were terrible circumstances however you look at it. There was no indication that HMS Cardiff could have known friendly aircraft were in the area that night. It is an awful fact that blue on blue happens in the heat of battle, fortunately and incredibly, this was the only aircraft blue on blue in the whole war.

June 6th was appalling weather and not much moved on either side till the movement of 5 Brigade with the Welsh and Scots Guards out of San Carlos.

The Argentinian Forces were not the only enemy in 1982, the weather was proving to be taken men out of the fight in more than could be afforded. Lt Colonel Nick Vaux, DSO, Commanding Officer 42 Commando, Royal Marines, accounted about just that, he said that 'the surroundings in which we now found ourselves were indeed a wilderness in the biblical sense. At times the terrain bore an eerie resemblance to the high moors of England, but at home the water table does not lie just a few inches below the surface. In the Falklands during winter, almost all the high ground is sodden with brackish water, rather than drained by fast flowing streams. Digging for cover creates a water filled ditch. Drinkable water is almost nonexistent. Provisions for survival had to be brought ashore, and then transported to the troops. But there were no roads beyond Stanley and the connecting settlement tracks were only passable to tracked vehicles or civilian tractors. On the higher ground, the steep slippery slopes, the swathes of jumbled boulders, or the buttresses of crags along the crest lines, made movement for laden men desperately exhausting and difficult, especially at night.' He goes on to say that the main problem now is the main part of an infantryman's being is his feet. No matter what the quality of footwear you have, eventually they are going to be soaked, the only way to keep your feet from getting trench foot was to keep them dry!! The threat of hypothermia was also a constant battle. We had to keep using foot powder and try keeping a pair of socks inside your clothing to get dry and change them about, not easy when it is constantly raining and wind chills bringing the temperature down to below freezing more often than not. Getting into a soaking wet sleeping bag to try drying things out isn't going to work. Whenever the opportunity could lend itself, we would take off the wet socks, apply foot powder, put on dry socks, then when we are ready to go again, put the wet socks back on in order to keep the dry socks for the next stop. The wind has what the met men call katabatic breezes, they continually change direction in many periods of time, defeating any effective siting of shelters from the wind chill. Each day brought blizzard, squall and downpour in relentless sequence. Occasionally the sun would break through providing temporary warmth and a precious chance to dry out any kit such as sleeping bags and socks. Wet feet are not just a situation that is inconvenient, when a foot is wet for long periods of time whilst walking, especially over the unforgiving terrain of the Falklands, the smallest grain of sand or dirt can cause the foot to blister, bleed or get infected, it becomes so painful that the toughest of soldiers cannot walk.

As they got closer to Stanley, the enemy were more and more concentrated, the mountains around the town had very dense strongholds and were heavily defended as their outer defenses, Two Sisters, Mt Harriet, Mt Longdon, Mt Tumbledown, Mt William, Wireless

Ridge and Sapper Hill. All had to be taken before the town of Stanley. The last four being closer to Stanley would be taken in the second stage of the British advance, the others were all detailed for capture on the night of 11/12 June, all had to be thoroughly checked for minefields and defensive positions before the assault. 45 Commando's Y Company sent out their recce patrol and a mortar section to give covering fire support in case of serious opposition. Things went tragically wrong when the patrol saw what they thought was an Argie patrol, they checked with Sgt Bob Leeming, the mortar commander. Sgt Leeming assured them that they were ready on high ground, the recce patrol were looking down on their quarry and felt confident that this was certainly an Argie patrol and opened fire, the awful truth was that they had fired on their own mortar team, killing Sgt Leeming, Cpls Pete Fitton and Andrew Uren, and Marine Keith Phillips.

To take the life of another human being, even in a war situation is a lifetime of psychological challenges. To take the lives of your friends?

Preparations were coming to an end for these Marine and Para Battalions, time was drawing closer to the beginning of the final push for these mountains. British artillery and naval guns started to pound the mountain tops to try to soften them up. 42 Commando were tying up loose ends, the commanders went to the Commanding Officer Lt Col Nick Vaux for final briefings before attacking Mt Harriet. The Argies sent in shells that overshot the Marines position but one hit the Mortar Platoon who was placing their base plates to prepare for the ensuing battle. The brittle granite rocks shattered into tiny fragments, Corporal Jeremy Smith was mortally wounded as a piece of fragment entered his heart, he died on the casevac helicopter out. Another, Marine Hagyard was cut open from the pelvis to the collar bone, he survived, and it was thought that he was the most serious casualty until the realisation of the aforementioned Corporal Smith. No one needed reminding about the treacherous night that lay ahead and the possibility of lives lost, but before the battle had begun, this was a huge blow to morale.

At the same time, over on Mt Longdon with 3 Para, Mt Longdon is a very narrow long ridge, it was decided that 3 Para, who were assigned this mission, could only use one Company to attack the ridge with the other two Companies attacking each side in support. It was going to be a "silent attack", this means that they will creep up as close as possible before all hell breaks loose. B Company was the Company tasked with attacking the ridge line. The Company Sergeant Major, John Weeks, had been with the Company for about two years and knew his men well, he got them together as the Commanders were being briefed and talked to them about their upcoming mission. He said, "It's going to be hand to hand fighting from trench to trench, it's going to be very very slow, and believe you me, you can't visualise what it's going to be like because it's going to be slow and you're going to have things happen that you've never had before when we've been practicing. You're going to have live things coming at you and exploding around you and it's going to confuse you. But you will do well. Now if you have any thoughts or you believe in Christ, here's the time to sit down and talk to Him. I'm not stupid because I'm certainly going to go away now and have a little prayer." He then called in his senior NCO's, he told them what he expected of them, he said "I don't expect anything less than what I would do, if you don't see me doing it, then you do it. I'm going to have enoughproblems supplying you with ammunition and everything else, without you causing me problems. Any problems with your Platoon Commanders, send them down to me and I'll sort the fuckers out!"

The start line was on the other side of a stream, called Furze Bush Pass Stream. The photo below shows the area today, bear in mind, in 1982 it was at night.

The small arrow is the start line. The large arrow is the Argie Commander Juan Baldini's command post overlooking the north west of the mountain, it was covered in tarpaulin and peat at the time. The crescent shape shows where the edge of a minefield is situated off the photo.

The start line is where an attacking force is formed up and everybody knows from that point it's the start of the business end, so to speak. In training and in some war situations, it's actually marked with white tape, this was not required here. When B Company moved through the rest of the battalion, friends were hugging and wishing them well, knowing that this could be the last time they would see each other again, tears were shed, this is real!

They crossed the start line on time, it was going well as they moved across the open ground leading up to the base of the crags. Corporal Brian Milne was on the left flank when he stepped on a mine, the silent attack is no more. There were more illuminations than Guy Fawkes Night or the 4th July, the thought was that most of the Argies had been asleep because had they been alert they would have wiped out half the Company. For the next 11 hours it was unbelievable nonstop action.

This shot was taken by a Para at the beginning when all hell broke loose.

An Argie mortar man defending the mountain wrote about his thoughts and account of the battle, he said that on the night of the battle he stood and looked down the western slope, he heard a clunk-click, then many clunk-clicks, it was the unmistakable sound of bayonets being fixed. Panic surged through his body, he ran to rouse the others, many who were sleeping. He shouted, "Get up, get up, the English are coming".

He then heard a loud bang then a scream, this was Cpl Milne stepping on the mine. Within seconds men were scrambling out of their bunkers, the whole place erupted with tracer bullets, whizzing past his head and thumping into the rocks and whizzing through the air as they ricocheted amongst the granite. Everyone was in a panic, he ran for cover and crawled into a bunker with a Sergeant, he couldn't fire his mortar now. Outside the English were running past screaming and firing into tents and bunkers. He could hear men being killed, they had only just woken up and now they were dying. He could hear muffled explosions followed by helpless cries, he knew grenades were being thrown into bunkers in the follow up. He and the Sgt suggested surrendering but decided to wait till it was over. All he could do was wait. The English were all around them. They had arrived in seconds, like lightening. He prayed a grenade would not come into his bunker. The sheer mental pressure exhausted him. He hated it.

Infantry tactics of fighting on the ground is called skirmishing, we work in teams whether it is two men or two groups, you work at "fire and maneuver". One team gives covering fire whilst the other team moves a few yards, takes cover and gives covering fire to the other team, this is very tiring work but effective. Working on the top of these mountains is extremely hard, negotiating rocks and crags, not knowing exactly where the enemy are is confusing. Eye witness accounts from this battle are frightening to read, to be a part of it.........!

The Regimental Aid Post (R.A.P.) was set up at the foot of the western slope, not far from where Cpl Milne was injured. The Paras skirmished forward into the Argie position, the first encounter Para on Argie was confusion of what to do next, the Paras were just looking at some two man tents and thinking of a Northern Ireland situation, there, you can only fire if you are fired upon! One of the Paras remembers saying to himself "Well, someone's got to start this fucking war". He zapped half a dozen rounds into the tents, he looked at his Sgt and he back at him and they realized that there's no turning back now. Things happen so quickly, bang......bang......bang. Some of the others looked at him as if he was mad, they didn't look for long because all hell had broken loose by now. The Argies had opened up from all angles at this point, it was very hard to determine where bullets were coming from, as the Paras skirmished through they missed some bunkers and were fired on from behind, taking cover all the while shouting to each other for information, trying to help each other out, looking in the dark for muzzle flashes. Some Argies gave up and were dragged off back to the R.A.P. A few guys were pinned down by a sniper and were being picked off, Cpl Trevor Wilson, L/Cpl James 'Doc' Murdoch and others couldn't move. Incoming rounds were coming in thick and fast, the smell of sulphur from the tracer rounds was thick in the air. Tony "Fester"

Greenwood got hit just above his left eye. Pete Grey had stood to throw a grenade and was shot in the forearm snapping it like a twig. 'Baz' Barrett went to get more field dressings to help Pete Grey, as he was coming back he was shot in the back. The snipers were just picking guys off. It was now obvious the snipers had extremely good night sights. There was no further they could go. It was very difficult and they suffered for it. They knew where the snipers were but every time they went to engage they had a round zing past their heads. Doc Murdoch was 'over there', there was nothing his mates could do, he was talking to them, telling them how he was, the sniper was toying with him, he was shot in the thigh first, then he was shot in the arm, then in the side of the head which blinded him. He was passing them all this information as he was being shot and dying, it is a terrible way to die, haunting. Cpl Jimmy Morham and Pte Stewart "Geordie" Laing decided that they were going to run and help Doc. Jimmy was removing his ammunition pouches to make it easier to move when someone shouted, "I'll cover you Geordie", Geordie got up and took three shots to the chest. He died instantly.

Pte Tony Kempster remembers at one point the battle was so intense under very very heavy fire that he was trying to dig himself into rocks, he said that if he so much as farted he feared he would be a goner. Suddenly, ahead of him he saw Cpl Stewart "Scouse" McLaughlin standing up on a rock, tracer (bullets that glow red burning sulphur) bullets everywhere, shouting, "C'mon lads, I'm fucking bullet proof, follow me!" The men did, on that mountain he was an inspiration to them all. Pte Kempster said that 'He found his hour'. Later on there was a huge explosion amongst some of the lads, it was believed to be a shell (as opposed to a rocket), Scouse McLaughlin was lying face down still alive having caught a large amount of the blast, he had a hole in his back about the size of a hand, his ribs, spine and internal organs were exposed. Pte Grant Grinham was shouting in pain, he had a horrendous leg injury, Lt Mark Cox administered morphine to him and called for a medic, from behind a rock a medic called back to him, Lt Cox said that he was coming over to him. Another huge explosion, when Lt Cox got to the medic he was dead against the rock. He grabbed his medic bag and went back to Grinham, many field dressings were administered to his leg. Stretcher bearers were called to take care of Cpl McLaughlin, he was complaining of sucking air (concerned about a lung injury) but was told he was going to be OK. A stretcher bearer took Grinham away, another, L/Cpl Peter Higgs came to help Cpl McLaughlin, he got him to his feet and was supporting him under his arms to get him back to the RAP. He had been fighting like a hero all night but now was saying 'My time is up', as he was being taken back to the RAP another shell came in and killed him. All of the evidence surrounding Cpl Scouse McLaughlin's bravery is unwavering, he was to be put up into the honours list, however, when he was being prepared for a body bag and later burial it was realised he had been cutting off the ears of Argies he had killed and he had been keeping them in his ammunition pouches. The intentions to award him with a bravery medal were quashed with this gruesome discovery.

The fighting was in such narrow confines with jagged rocks all around, it was very difficult to push on, snipers and bunkers everywhere. Three machine gun nests were doing a lot of damage and they were holding up the advance. Sgt Ian Mackay, one of the Platoon Sergeants decided someone had to do something about them, he took 3 Privates (known in the Paras as 'Toms') and Cpl Ian Bailey, they needed to push on 30-35 yards to these next bunkers, they charged, 2 of the Toms were killed straight away, the other managed to make it to the next cover, they grenaded the first bunker and ran through firing into it as they went without stopping. Cpl. Bailey got shot in the hip and went down, he saw Sgt Mackay still running forward firing but could not see anyone else with him. Sgt McKay got to one of the machine gun nests killing all in there but losing his life at the same time.

With B Company encountering heavy resistance on the top, A company had moved through on the left flank, the northern ridge without much trouble, they wanted to engage the Argies from their position down below the summit but couldn't risk hitting their own men. They could make out where snipers were though through the red light on their night sights. They were able to take out these snipers from this lower position until the Argies figured it out and were now engaging A Company from higher ground. The Company Commanders signaller Cpl Steve Hope was hit by a sniper, he died of his injuries on the hospital ship SS Uganda the following day. Pte Timothy Jenkins made the fatal mistake of peering too long to look for these snipers and was swiftly picked off.

Support Company's heavy machine guns were now used to put sustained fire into a lot of these positions, the men on the ground were also using 66mm anti-tank guns to fire the rockets into bunkers.

As A Company were moving into their flanking position, Major Mike Argue, B Company Commander tasked 2 platoons and some Support Company to use an outflanking maneuver along a sheep track that ran on the northern slope just below the summit. Lt Mark Cox led them along the track, as it was so narrow they had to move in single file. They rounded a bend and came across an Argie patrol, Lt Cox and his signaller Pte Steve Phillips dived out of the way shouting out a warning as they did. The men behind caught most of the firepower which killed Pte Jonathan Crow and wounded L/Cpl Lennie Carver and Pte Frank Reagan. The patrol could not return fire as the Argies ran off. A call to Company HQ requesting for a fire mission on the location of the Argies resulted in the Artillery forward observation officer Capt. Willie

McCracken firing a 66mm Anti-Tank gun at them, it must have hit the ammunitions one of them was carrying because it resulted in an almighty flash. A flurry of grenades and rifle fire from the Paras resulted in the elimination of the Argie ambush group. The group pressed on. They alighted the ridge and were immediately under fire again from more defensive positions, Pte Dominic Gray was hit in the head and knocked a short distance down the hill, he took off his helmet and felt blood running down his face and neck, the helmet had a hole in each side and his head had a neat groove in the hairline. Somehow the helmet and liner had deflected the bullet thus saving his life. He still cherishes the helmet today as a reminder how close he came to losing his life.

B Company had done as much and gone as far as they could go. Lt Col Hew Pike, Commanding Officer 3 Para decided that he should have A Company now take over, the Argies were not as easy to convince to give up than was first thought. Bunkers were thought to have been taken out only to start up again when Paras were in the open thinking areas were clear. B Company handed all their belted machine gun ammunition to A Company lads. Men went forward in attacking mode taking cover behind rocks as they went. Communication was now by shouting. When a soldier could see a position he would light a cigarette so that our guys could see him, he would then give an indication from where his lit cigarette was to the next manned bunker, fire would be put down on there until the target was hit accurately, then it would be hammered, firing about 200 to 300 rounds into it. They moved about 100 yards in an hour, taking out about 8 bunkers along the way. This was still only the first group of positions.

To the rear of the main battle was the Corps of Drums Machine Gun crews and the Anti-Tank platoon of Support Company, when the battle seemed to all be going the way of A Company up front, a 105mm shell from a 105mm Recoilless rifle flew onto the mountain from (believed to be) Wireless Ridge, which is located on the other side of the ridge of Mt Longdon, a sort of continuation towards the other side of the Stanley Harbour. The shell flew in between Capt. Tony Mason, OC Anti-Tank Platoon, and Peter Dennison, it exploded behind them into a Milan Anti-Tank guided weapon system and its crew, killing Cpl Keith 'Ginge' McCarthy, Pte Philip West and Pte Peter Hedicker. They were all literally blown to pieces with a direct hit. Cpl Jimmy Morham tried to give Ginge McCarthy mouth to mouth, it was too much for Ginge. The memories for those men were the smell of morphine and blood, memories that will stay with them forever.

The 105mm Recoilless Rifle believed to be the one that killed the Milan Section on Longdon. Wheels have been since removed, probably by Falkland Islanders after the war as spares. Two Sisters in the background.

During this horrific time of battle on Mt Longdon, shelling came and went, they could now tell when it was our shells that were fired towards the Argies and the Argies shells being fired at them. At one time some boys were in a bunker taking cover from a session of shelling, (there was normally about 30 mins between shelling) after one bout that had come in, one of the lads pulled out a packet of hot chocolate, he kept it for an occasion like this, you never know when your next resupply is going to be, he said 'let's brew one up, there's 30 mins before the next shells'. They got out the burner and a metal mug on top of it and were lovingly looking at it brewing when they heard a BOOM...BOOM...BOOM, one of them thought 'Oh fucking hell', the other one said, "it's OK, it's one of ours" then – WHOOOSH! KERBAMBBB! "Fucking Hell" he said, "quick, get yer 'elmet off", the one grabbed the helmet and put it over the drinking chocolate to save dust dropping in it from the roof of the bunker, the other said "you knock that over and I'll never fucking speak to you again."

Morning broke and the last resisting pockets of enemy were either killed or taken as prisoners. As I mentioned earlier at the end of the Goose Green battle, the dead have to be accounted for and recorded. There are no follow up teams to do this, the guys have to take care of their friends, these friends they were having a cuppa with or some banter not 24 hrs before. CSM John Weeks explains it best; it's his job to arrange this and asks for volunteers. It's not something you can order the boys to do. Some lads make excuses that they are busy doing something else because they don't want to see their friend's dead bodies, certainly not in some of the gruesome demises that some suffered. All these boys had to be checked, recording their wounds and remove personal effects like wedding rings, photos, wallets and the like. One dog tag taken and one left on. Then they have to put them onto a poncho and carry them to a central location, in this case the RAP, put them into heavy duty plastic body bags for later burial. These Paras were taken to be temporarily buried at Teale Inlet as mentioned earlier, later to be either buried in San Carlos or back home on the British mainland in a local or military cemetery. 23 Airborne Soldiers from 3rd Battalion Parachute Regiment were killed on Mt Longdon.

36 Argentines were killed but were found to have little or no identification. They are buried in the Argentine cemetery in Darwin.

Argentinian 105mm Recoilless Rifle on Mt Longdon.

View of the type of terrain on Mt Longdon.

White arrow showing two of our group as a guide to size.

3 Para memorials, Mt Longdon.

Mt Longdon. A view of where the British advance
was coming from.

Sgt Ian John McKay VC. There are 23 bronze poppies on this granite rock representing each of the soldiers that lost their lives on Mt Longdon.

More 3 Para Memorials Mt Longdon

More 3 Para Memorials, Mt Longdon

50mm Machine gun nests on Mt Longdon, an idea of the type of fighting terrain.

Another Machine gun nest   An idea of how narrow this

fighting ridge was

Mt Longdon overlooking Stanley.

Around about the same time as 3 Para were entering this battle, 45 Commando, Royal Marines were ascending Two Sisters. (42 Commando were also in the midst of fighting on Mt Harriett) These men were heading for the top of Two Sisters, 1 Troop were to attack the right hand peak whilst the other two Companies were to take out the left hand peak, only these men can fully know what it must have been like. Before they came under fire from the Argies they could see across to Mt Longdon and Mt Harriet at the battles that were in full flow over there, there were bombs, flares and tracer everywhere. They were told by one of the Commanders, Capt. Gardiner that they must keep fighting through, if anyone falls, their body must be marked, even if it's just sticking their rifle into the ground so that the follow up teams can identify they are ours and not the enemies bodies. With the sophisticated weaponry these days, identification can be difficult.

These Marines had actually been based at the lower slopes of Mt Kent for a week since June 4th, liaising with British Special Air Service they mounted several patrols gathering loads of information about the Argies based on top of Two Sisters. This gave them a big advantage going into the night of the 11th.

The Marines on the left hand peak came under fire first, the right hand peak took a little longer because the Argies were further to the top, there were no enemy on the first 2 objectives as they ascended. One of the lads said, 'perhaps there is nobody here', as if on cue a wall of tracer came at them from the top, all hell broke loose. As they fired and maneuvered through the rocks they saw several dead Argie bodies that had been there for days. A fighting patrol had been here about four days before and they just left their bodies there. They were now under immense fire lying among these bodies. To their detriment, the Argies opened fire too early, they couldn't really see the Marines, they just knew they were there somewhere, their fire wasn't having any effect, and most was going over their heads. The Argie that organized these mountains however was pretty switched on, he had every route up channeled to a heavy machine gun. This meant the Marines were pretty much pinned down for a lot of the time. To put your head up above these rocks would have meant it would probably have been shot off. Suddenly one of the Troop Commanders grabbed three men and shouted, 'follow me boys'. He got up and ran into a gully firing his rifle, this was leading into a heavy machine gun, about ten seconds later he came running back! Change of plan. He never tried that again!

There was also rifle fire in amongst all this heavy machine gun fire coming down at them. Dave O'Connor, one of the Marines machine gunners decided to leap forward with his number 2 carrying his belts of ammunition out in the open and got on a rock and opened fire at their machine gun. It was a battle of the big guns at each other. A young Marine jumped up with a 66mm Anti-Tank gun and fired it at the

117

machine gun, it exploded above the position, he stood there waiting for another 66 to be thrown up to him, he armed it and fired again, this time it hit close and the firing stopped for a split second, that was the key for the attack to start up again, they got across the ridge and moved up towards the enemy in very fast speed. The Argies then started to retreat leaving bodies and weapons behind. The Marines took out the machine guns and other small pockets, they then moved toward the other peak, throwing grenades into the bunkers, then following up with rifle fire till all positions were cleared.

Not much has been documented about this battle even though the bravery and skill of these Marines made quick work of their success, it seems to have been under-represented in post war publications. Three Marines lost their lives during this battle, Cpl Ian Spencer, Marine Michael Nowak and Marine Gordon Mcpherson, also Sapper Chris Jones of 59 Independent Commando Sqn, Royal Engineers. All are buried in the UK.

HMS Glamorgan was off shore giving fire support to the Marines on Two Sisters during the night, firing shells from 6-7 miles away and landing within 200 metres of our own troops. At the end of the battle Glamorgan was preparing to leave her position when they spotted a blip on the radar heading towards them. They had been shelled by Argie Howitzers all night but with no effect. This was different, it had a flare behind it, they knew now it was an exocet missile, designed to strike a ship at the water line, they had exactly 10 seconds to react, the Navigating Officer of his own volition turned the ship so its stern was showing, leaving the exocet with the smallest target as possible. The exocet hit and flew upwards through the deck exploding. A refueled helicopter was also hit which caused a huge fire, burning fuel ran down into the galley killing the men inside. 13 men lost their lives in that attack but the ship was not lost, the only ship to survive an exocet missile strike through the quick thinking of the crew.

For the next few days the Marines had to take cover in amongst the rocks as they were bombarded by Argie Artillery and mortar fire.

The battle for Mt Harriet was the other of the three battles due to take place that night. 42 Commando, Royal Marines had this mission. Several pieces of intelligence gathering had taken place preceding this attack, in particular, Sgt Michael Collins was on a fact finding patrol when he came across an Argie patrol, he subdued his men into not fighting with this patrol, instead they followed it back to their position on Mt Harriet. Lt Col Nick Vaux's plan was to move to the east of the mountain, bearing in mind they are coming from a north westerly direction to it, thus skirting around to almost the far side as shown on the map below. Zoya was the codename for Harriet after one of Lt Col Vaux's daughters. The red markings plotted post war are minefields.

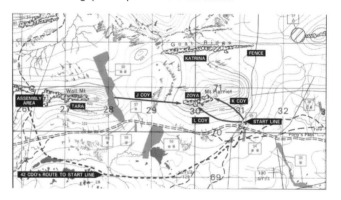

The start line, which is where the plaque (photos on pages 124 and 125) is placed now, would not have been an expected attack position, J Company were to make a diversionary firefight on Wall Mountain (Tara) to the west of Mt Harriet, the direction the British were expected to fight from.

K and L Companies were to attack from the east, K Company to attack the right hand side and 30 minutes later L Company were to attack the left hand side, there is a distinct saddle in the middle which was to act as an inter-company boundary. K Company were ready to move off the start line and found out that L Company were late, a Recce Platoon were supposed to locate the start line ahead of them but, it is said that they got the wrong location! K Company moved off and was within 100 metres from the top before the enemy were engaged. Some of the men were walking in amongst Argie tents before they were even noticed. A shot rang out, a Corporal shouted, "who fired that" then all hell broke loose and there were bullets flying everywhere, fire and maneuver, take cover, get up and shoot, get behind a rock…. Whilst all this was going on there were mortars and machine gun fire coming from the Argies. Some of the men were pinned down by a sniper, Cpl Steve Newland thought he could crawl around and find this sniper to take him out, he managed to get within a short throwing distance and then saw him, the sniper was not the only one there, there were about 10 others all lined up laying on a flat piece of rock, also a machine gun crew. They were waiting for the guys to come out into the open to try to take out the sniper then they would all open up. He pulled pins from 2 grenades, he threw one straight at the gun team and the other in amongst the rifles and sniper, when both went off he got up and attacked firing a whole magazine of 20 rounds. He thought he had killed them when over his radio he was told that his colleagues down the hill were about to fire two 66mm into the enemy, he told them to wait and ran back down to a rock gulley, he told them to fire, the two 66's exploded. He was told to go back and clear up, by now he has put another magazine onto his rifle and went back, one of the Argies was only hit in the shoulder and opened up with an automatic hitting him in the legs. He was so angry at being caught out after all that, that he emptied a mag into this guy. He now had to figure out how to get back. There were bullets still flying everywhere and bombs exploding. He felt his legs stiffen to a point that he stood and started walking back down like Frankenstein's monster. He discarded his rifle just in case his colleagues thought he was the enemy, he was stopped by a Marine who said, "Halt, who's that?" he said "Steve Newland, somebody come and get me, I've been hit in the legs" He was rescued and eventually taken back down the mountain to wait for medics.

As the Marines were pushing through hiding behind rocks, lying amongst dead Argies, one of the guys, Tony Koleszar, thought that a dead Argie next to him had a good pair of boots and his were worn out, he started taking them off the Argie when he sat up, they both had a huge fright. Shots were fired into the Argie from everywhere, Tony decided he didn't want the boots anymore.

L Company had now joined in the fight and were shooting from down the mountain up at it, they were precariously close to their own men and had to be warned off to stop shooting, K Company were being fired at from all sides. L Company eventually ascended and joined in the fight to the summit. Along the way during these skirmishes, Cpl Laurence Watts was killed, the only fatality for 42 Commando that night.

Another Argie machine gun team was holding up another part of the attack for a long time, they were so well dug into the mountainside that hundreds of bullets were not having any effect. L/Cpl John Mahoney and his Milan (guided anti-tank gun) team mate from the Welsh Guards Kevin Sincock came forward and fired into the bunker taking it out. The attack was now able to advance further.

The next morning after the final Argies surrendered, the job of finding all their bodies, collecting their identification and then burying them had to be done, all of this under artillery bombardment from the Argies. By now few of these men even ducked when a shell came in and exploded, they just looked to where the explosion was and just carried on.

The start line as indicated on page 120

The top of Mt Harriet with Mt Tumbledown in the distance
and Port Stanley beyond that.

June 13th. Preparations were being made for the final attacks
of the war before the push into Stanley, Mt Tumbledown was to be
taken by the Scots Guards. The Gurkhas were to work around the
north side of Tumbledown and attack Mt William. The Welsh Guards
number 2 Company and an attachment of Royal Marines were to

attack Sapper Hill. The Argies that had retreated from the mountains liberated by the British were now assembled on Tumbledown, many of them Special Forces.

The Argies were still pounding the mountains that were successfully taken by British Forces. My dear friend Bowser was killed during this time, hence the confusion whether he was killed by a shell or a land mine.

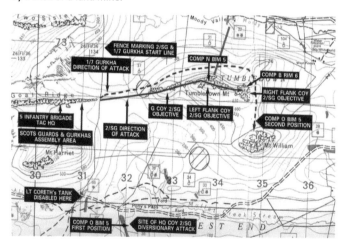

The attack on Tumbledown was to take place around midnight of 13/14 June. To the south was a diversionary attack, the direction the

Argies were expecting to be hit from. Drill Sgt Danny Wight and two other soldiers, L/Cpl John Pashley of the Royal Engineers and another Guardsman came across a sentry bunker at the site of this attack, they thought the sentry must have been sleeping and got to within 3 feet, he fired at the British soldiers, Danny Wight was hit and killed instantly, L/Cpl Pashley was hit in the throat and later died and the Guardsman was hit in the arm. A firefight of about ten minutes ensued finally overpowering the sentry position, 7 injured Guardsmen, 2 killed and 10 dead Argies. The Scots Guards knew they were going to be in for a very hard night.

Simple crosses for Drill Sgt Danny Wight and L/Cpl John Pashley.

The attack on Tumbledown was certainly a difficult task, the plan was to advance by sending in G Company first to take out the first objective, the west end of the mountain. Once that had been taken, Left Flank Company would leapfrog them and take out the first peak, Right Flank Company then to leapfrog and take out the east end final peak. G Company were supported by canon fire from the Blues and Royals armoured vehicles, the first objective was taken fairly easily as there was no one really there.

Left Flank Company leapfrogged and was coming under immense firepower, they were pinned down for a long time, anti-tank guns were used to fire at the bunkers that the Argies were heavily dug into, when a shell exploded the rest of the platoons would fire into that explosion. They could only move forward very slowly. Still the Argies had strong positions and continued to have the advantage on firepower. The Scots Guards used Artillery to pound at the enemy positions, after 2 hours of stalemate they decided that at the end of the third salvo of shelling they would mount a surprise attack on the enemy, this strategy worked, finally taking out the last of the Argies on the first peak. When they reached the peak, the Company Commander Major Kiszley, Lt Mitchell and five others realized they were finally at the top, they could actually see Stanley down below, street lights on and vehicles moving along the roads. As they stood looking down at this final view they were fired upon by a group of Argies below them, Lt Mitchell was hit in the legs and others were also wounded. A stretcher party eventually got to them and managed to start moving back down the mountain. One of the stretcher party, Guardsman James Reynolds was actually shot in the arm before he got to help Lt Mitchell but managed to carry the stretcher with his good arm. The injured men had to be carried over extremely rough terrain to get back down the mountain for medical repairs. At one point whilst they were in the open, it appears that a mortar group from an Argie position, probably on neighbouring Sapper Hill saw them and fired their mortars, some rounds landed about 200-300 yds away, one landed right on top of them, two of the stretcher party were killed instantly, literally blown to pieces, one sadly was Gdsm Reynolds, the other was his close friend Gdsm David Malcolmson. Lt Mitchell knowing there was nothing he could do for those men had to get himself and the other wounded down without the use of a stretcher, he used a rifle as a crutch and the help of Gdsm Findlay. Gdsm Reynolds was later posthumously awarded the Distinguished Conduct Medal, it was presented by his family to the Scots Guards where it is now on display in the conference room of the Scots Guards HQ.

Right Flank Company now leap frogged Left Flank in order to

attack the final east end peak of Mt Tumbledown. They were immediately pinned down by heavy machine gun fire. They decided to attack it around the right side, as they pushed around, the mountain fell away so they were below the machine gun post, they couldn't work out the exact location. They asked Left Flank Company to help with supporting fire and direct their own weapons onto the position. Lt Robert Lawrence decided that getting close to this position is really the only way to take it out, he crawled with grenade in hand and when he threw it, he called for the rest of his platoon to follow up, he was very excited when he saw every man get up and charge the machine gun. This turned out to be three machine guns and another further on. In the dark and confusion some enemy soldiers were missed, either because they were not seen or they pretended to be dead. At some stage the Scots Guards were being fired on from the rear also. Lt Lawrence was hit in the head exposing a large part of his brain. Captain Sam Drennan of the Army Air Corps, flying a Scout helicopter, (as it happens was in fact a Colour Sergeant with the Scots Guards before he transferred to the Air Corps) was told that Scots Guards casualties needed to be casevac'd off Mt Tumbledown, he along with his observer L/Cpl Julian "Jay" Rigg flew into enemy fire to achieve this on more than one occasion, one of these casualties was Lt Lawrence, he was taken to Fitzroy field hospital where he was treated for his wounds.

Several hours of attack, take cover, attack, take cover as the Argies continually fired their last gasp mortars and artillery onto the final positions of Tumbledown. The last enemy surrender was around 7:30 in the morning. The Argie Commander started with 45 Marines on that last peak, he ended up with 13. It was a long and hard battle.

Scots Guards memorial on top of Mt Tumbledown

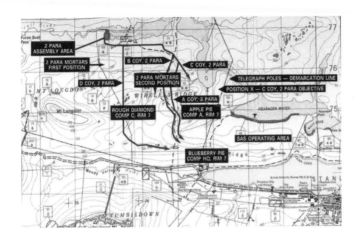

As the battles for Mt Tumbledown and Mt William were to be getting under way, 2 Para were preparing for their second battle of the war on Wireless Ridge overlooking Port Stanley. As the map above shows, the ridge was split into 3 names, the first was Rough Diamond which D Company would attack first, when that was successful they would move on to Blueberry Pie. A and B Companies would then attack Apple Pie. Each of these battles were intense with small arms fire but all the while the enemy were retreating, the fighting continued through the night until the enemy finally surrendered.

During the end of the battle the Paras could see the Argies leaving Mt Tumbledown and thought they were on their way to reinforce Sapper Hill, they arranged artillery fire down on them.

Mt William which was to be attacked by the Gurkhas had already retreated and that was taken with ease as was Sapper Hill. Over the radio were the words "white flags have been seen flying over Stanley" The Argentinian Forces had finally accepted defeat and surrendered.

Wireless Ridge with Stanley in the distance

Argentine trench on Sapper Hill

Inside the same Argentine trench on Sapper Hill

Ben Parry, Jimmy Everett, Ronnie Mackenzie, Bill Mott, Chris Hopkins and me on the top of Sapper Hill with the mountain ranges of battle sites in the background.

THE SURRENDER

The end was inevitable. General Mendez was speaking with the Argentinian leader, General Galtieri back on the mainland, the discussion of surrender was talked about, Galtieri wanted him to fight to the end. Mendez did not want any more of his brave men to die and therefore, hating to do it, he decided to surrender. Little did anyone know at the time but the British Forces were at the end of their rope, ships and aircraft were in desperate need of repairs and refits, the troops were in much need of rest, it has been said that the Royal Artillery were down to their last shell before the surrender.

Major-General Jeremy Moore was flown into Stanley. The surrender document had been prepared, it did have 'unconditional' surrender. Mendez wanted that word taken out, so that his officers could be giving up with dignity, they were allowed to keep their weapons to take back to Argentina with them. General Mendez signed the document at midnight on the 14th June, 8pm UK time.

Headquarters, Land Forces
Falkland Islands

INSTRUMENT OF SURRENDER

I, the undersigned, Commander of all the Argentine land, sea and air forces in the Falkland Islands unconditionally surrender to Major General J. J. MOORE CB OBE MC* as representative of Her Brittanic Majesty's Government.

Under the terms of this surrender all Argentinian personnel in the Falkland Islands are to muster at assembly points which will be nominated by General Moore and hand over their arms, ammunition, and all other weapons and warlike equipment as directed by General Moore or appropriate British officers acting on his behalf.

Following the surrender all personnel of the Argentinian Forces will be treated with honour in accordance with the conditions set out in the Geneva Convention of 1949. They will obey any directions concerning movement and in connection with accommodation.

This surrender is to be effective from 2359 hours ZULU on 14 June (2059 hours local) and includes those Argentine Forces presently deployed in and around Port Stanley, those others on East Falkland, Colonia, West Falkland and all the outlying islands.

.... Commander Argentine Forces

.... J. J. MOORE
Major General

.... Witness

.... hours   June 1982

Unlike too many heroes of the Falklands War, we returned to the Lodge in Stanley, we got ready and went to Tim and Jan Miller's for dinner. Wonderful hosts and a delicious dinner, all produce grown from their gardens. The Miller's are the main producers of vegetables and fruit for the islands and cruise ships that come in almost every day.

After dinner we created the 8 + 2 group, eight Welsh Guards and 2 others, Ronnie Mackenzie, Scots Guards and Smokey Cole, Royal Navy. This was a poignant name as we are remembering the war of '82. We decided Ronnie would be first chairman and that we would try to meet up each year.

The Miller's house has a large dedication to everything Welsh, they have a Welsh flag that we, along with several Welshmen before us signed, it is used every year on St David's Day (Welsh St Paddy's day) and June 8th at the memorial at Fitzroy.

We returned to the lodge for banter jokes, more beer and bed.

Monday 4th Feb, 2013

Today we went to Fitzroy for a memorial service at the Welsh Guards memorial site, we were to go out onto the water to lay a wreath at the site of the attack on RFA Sir Galahad, I was afforded the extremely high honour of laying the wreath on the water, this apparently has never been done before. The weather was so bad it would have been too dangerous to go out, we held the memorial at the cross instead. The very strong wind made everyone's eyes water….a lot…..it was a very moving experience and service. Lots of man hugs followed and strong emotional memories were had, I laid the wreath at the base of the Celtic Cross. This was shipped from Wales out of Welsh rock.

Welsh Guards Memorial, Fitzroy.

Reads.. 'Sir Galahad, take care of our brothers, the Welsh Guards, as you have done for the past 30 years, Welsh Guards Veterans'

We were taken to and shown the shearing sheds that we were given medical aid after the attack on the Galahad, unfortunately the wind was so strong that when I opened the back door to get my rucksack, the wind took the door out of my hand and swung open at a very fast speed, walking alongside the van was Charlie Carty who "met" the back door with his eye. Sorry Charlie!! BIG black eye followed.

We returned to Stanley and walked around the town that afternoon, Billy and Nick showed me some points of interest and where they stayed after the war.

Bill and Nick Mott outside the Police Station

The Police Station after Royal Naval shelling of Stanley in 1982.

Bill and I outside the Police Station.

Inside the Town Hall where they lived after the war.

Bill in his old bed space.

Nick in his old bed space.

Falklands Liberation Memorial reads
"In memory of those who liberated us 14th June 1892"

Street scenes of Stanley.

That evening we went to a couple's house for dinner, Ian and Shirley, they run the fishing industry around the Falkland Islands. Ian is from Scotland and has been there for 20 years, he used to work for a 'flat pack housing' company, he built these in the Falklands and ended up staying, his house is a finished 'flat pack' with swimming pool. He now runs his own flat pack business on the Island. Lovely food and company.

Tuesday 5th Feb, 2013

Today we went to battle sites that I have previously explained about, all close to Stanley and the run in battles to the surrender, our guide explained the routes and surrender.

The evening took us to local pubs for dinner and some laughter. One of the pubs had a toilet seat on the wall with a photo of General Galtieri in the middle, nice picture frame.

During our time at the lodge we had occasion to visit the local store for supplies and phone cards, one of the girls that work there asked why we were here, we explained and by sheer coincidence, her father or grandfather, who now lives in Stanley, used to live in Fitzroy, he was helping us to move equipment and ammunition around in the area during the war as he had the only tractor available. I arranged for him to come to one of the pubs to meet us. When he arrived on this night, this wonderful man, George Butler, now in his 80's was introduced to the group, some of the guys that were not injured on the Galahad remember him helping us, what an amazing meeting.

Back to the lodge for after dinner drinks, banter and bed.

Wed 6th Feb, 2013

Today we drove for 2 hours to the furthermost point on East Falkland, the NW tip of the Island, we had lunch at our guide's summer cottage and went to the coast to visit penguins, I got some great shots but was a little disappointed not to see emperor penguins, they were not at home.

Genetos penguins.

Who's curious.....human or penguin??

We arrived back at the lodge and got dressed to go to dinner at the local hotel, the Malvina, named after the Scottish owner's daughter, nothing to do with the islands in Argentinian. Billy presented some plaques to some of the Islanders that were recognised for their contribution and help to the veterans over the years.

<u>Thursday 7th Feb, 2013</u>

George Butler came to the lodge and escorted myself Ben Parry and Nick Mott to Fitzroy to show us his side of what he remembers of the 8th June 1982. I walked back onto the beach where I came ashore on that fateful day, very moving with horrible memories but cathartic in it's moment.

We spent the afternoon relaxing and preparing to leave the next day. We walked down to a local pub for dinner and beer, returned and early to bed (for a change).

In the lodge are several books, one of which was a note book dating back to 1982 during the war, it's a book from the Quartermaster of the Scots Guards, he was providing soldiers hot dogs as they went through his position, (the story is something like that anyway) as I was reading it, my jaw dropped when I read the following.

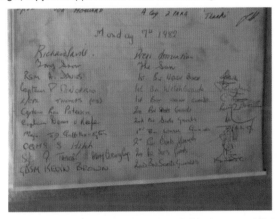

There in his own handwriting and his unmistakable signature, L/Cpl Thomas 03, my best friend stopped for a hotdog.

Friday 8th Feb, 2013

Leave the Lodge at 6.30am to Air Force base. When we got above the clouds the pilot informed us we have a couple that want to say goodbye to us. SUPERB, unfortunately I only had my phone camera and not my main.

We arrived back in Brize Norton early the next day, long and tiring trip, but very well worth it.

POSTFACE

The toils of war are unforgiving, men and women fight around the world, not because they want to, because it is a job, it is because we believe in our freedom. No person has the right to enslave a free people from their birth right. When we were told we were going to the Falklands, I along with many soldiers were very proud to be going, we were going to free British people from a foreign dictator.

My shooting team coach at that time was a man I greatly admired and looked up to, Company Sergeant Major Brian "Ernie" Pritchard, (since passed away). He was from the elite Guards Parachute Regiment and proudly wore his airborne wings with honour. He had seen a lot in his day and said to us 'you do not want to be going down there, trust me'.

Constant training in battlefield situations and shooting at wooden targets every day is like practicing a sport such as football or rugby but never being able to play a game against opposition. Now we can put that practice into reality. The time has come to defend our nation against an oppressor and we are ready for it. It's not a glory hunt or anything like that, as I said at the beginning, they fly the British flag and they drink British beer, that's good enough for me.

If anyone said they weren't scared, they are lying, worried?....not a bit. It's a different thing, even though we knew going down there we would be out numbered 6-1, we knew that we are better trained than they are and those odds seemed fair.

I wanted to name the book '30 YEARS OF BATTLE' because of the length of time that has passed since the war in 1982 to the re-visit. Hardly a day has passed in those 30 years that I have not thought about that war and the horror it brought. I think the re-visit helped a little to lay ghosts to rest, but I think it is the burden I have to bear for the rest of my life after returning and leaving so many behind, but I am OK with that.

Ernie Pritchard's words still resonate with me to this day, if I had to do it all over again I would not miss a beat, I would do it tomorrow.

RIP fallen heroes

Live in peace the families of those lost, in the knowledge it was not in vain.

RIP Baroness Thatcher, LG OM PC FRS

The Falkland Islands are, and will be forever British.

Acknowledgements

Lt Col (Retired) Tony Davies, OBE, MBE., without whom this journey would never have taken place.

The SAS raid on the airfield at Pebble Island. Courtesy of the Royal Air Force website, History of the RAF, The Falkland Islands campaign.

Falkland Island maps; Courtesy of "The Falklands War, Then and Now" by Gordon Ramsay

All first hand eye witness accounts; courtesy of "The Falklands War, then and Now" by Gordon Ramsay

Photos of RFA Sir Galahad after being hit courtesy of "The Falklands War, then and Now" by Gordon Ramsay and The Falklands Islands War museum.

Photo of me after coming ashore courtesy of BBC clip taken from You Tube.

Original photo of troops coming ashore on the San Carlos jetty; from the Falkland Islands War museum.

Surrender document courtesy of "The Falklands War, then and Now" by Gordon Ramsay.

Reviews

We have always been very close as a brother and sister with only just over a year between us. I hated the time that you were away in 1982 but was also very very proud of you Bowser and others who I had got to know quite well at that time. As a family this was a very tough time for us too as we had no idea most of the time of what was going on and where you were - I remember June 8, 1982 as if it were yesterday. The emotions and fear that we went through once we had received a phone call to tell us that you had been involved in the incident as Bluff Cove remains as clear in my mind now as it was then. As your sister I felt that I went through all the emotions with you at that time, but now, having read your book, I realised my emotions were so different to the ones that you were going through. The book is a very interesting read for me. I can now see that the pain and anguish you went through at that time, I will never be able to comprehend. The book was tough for me to read I cried, I smiled and I remembered.I am so proud of you Andrew, but I'm also very sorry that at such a young age you had to endure what you did in 1982.

RIP Bowser - I still smile fondly when I think of you !

Kay Brinkworth.

I thought it was great! Obviously a very moving experience for you...both times in the Falklands! What came across was how relationships formed in battle are very special... and last a lifetime.

You are fortunate, indeed, that you got through it safely. I can only imagine what it is like to see a comrade die next to you in battle.

I think you did a very commendable job writing! The pictures, too, help the reader envision what happened. Good choice of pictures. This was a history lesson for me! I learned about the Falklands War, and about you.

I hope you will share this with others who were there.

It's good stuff, Andy. As they say, there is a book in all of us!

Will Freeman, Professor, Grinnell College, Iowa.

.... what a book this is.

There are things in here that I knew vaguely about but your work expands it and to the extent of names, very interesting reading.

Again, your photographic work shows exactly what you're talking about. I really found your work very informative and compelling. You've obviously spent a lot of time researching and it shows.

Garrison Sergeant Major (London District) Bill Mott, OBE, MVO

I have read your book again and again and cannot tell you how close I feel to it all. What a really good job you have done in putting it all together. Well done mate, a good tribute to your best mate to those that read it.

Lt. Col (Retired) Tony Davies, MBE. OBE

Printed in Great Britain
by Amazon